Zookeeper

Written by
Douglas S. Haynes

Illustrated by
Daniel J. Middleton

Old Stone Press

Zookeeper
By Douglas S. Haynes

Illustrated by Daniel J. Middleton

Published by Old Stone Press
an imprint of J. H. Clark & Associates, Inc.
Louisville, Kentucky 40207 USA
www.oldstonepress.com

© 2018, Douglas S. Haynes

All rights reserved.

No part of this book may be reproduced in whole or in part without the written permission from the publisher, Old Stone Press, or the author, Douglas S. Haynes, except by a reviewer who may quote brief passages in a review or articles for publication.

For information about special discounts for bulk purchases or autographed copies of this book, please contact J. H. Clark, Old Stone Press at john@oldstonepress.com or the author, Douglas S. Haynes at dshenterprises01@gmail.com

Zookeeper
By Douglas S. Haynes

Library of Congress Control Number: 2018954688
ISBN: 978-1-938462-34-4

Published in the United States

This is dedicated to my daughter Carson, whose journey to college unleashed in me an urgency to offer advice. She hung this poem on her freshman dorm wall.

Zookeeper

You are your own zookeeper.

Nurture your pets.

Be a turtle,

and you will always be at home.

Be a bird,

fly above problems
and avoid snakes.

Be a puppy.

Be glad to see everybody.

Be a fish.

Move smoothly
in the swarm.

Awareness brings rewards and safety.

Be a tame night owl.

Be a lightning bug.

Let your loved ones know where you are.

Be an elephant.

www.ingramcontent.com/pod-product-compliance
Lightning Source LLC
Chambersburg PA
CBHW040618300426
43661CB00148B/1325/J